T. B. Odeneal

The Modoc War

Statement of Its Origin and Causes ....

T. B. Odeneal

The Modoc War
Statement of Its Origin and Causes ....

ISBN/EAN: 9783337010157

Printed in Europe, USA, Canada, Australia, Japan

Cover: Foto ©ninafisch / pixelio.de

More available books at **www.hansebooks.com**

THE

MODOC WAR;

STATEMENT

OF ITS

ORIGIN AND CAUSES,

CONTAINING

AN ACCOUNT OF THE TREATY, COPIES OF PETITIONS, AND OFFICIAL CORRESPONDENCE.

PORTLAND, OREGON:

"BULLETIN" STEAM BOOK AND JOB PRINTING OFFICE.

1873.

Hon. T. B. ODENEAL,

Superintendent Indian Affairs, Salem, Oregon,

SIR: Owing to the many erroneous impressions made upon the press and people of the Atlantic States, by the numerous false accounts given by newspaper correspondents of the present trouble with the Indians in southern Oregon, we would respectfully request that you furnish, for publication, a statement from the records in your possession, of all facts pertaining to the origin, cause, and commencement of the existing difficulties with the Modoc Indians. We are impelled to make this request only by a sincere desire to shield the State from injury by the erroneous publications referred to.

H. W. SCOTT,
C. P. CRANDALL,
B. GOLDSMITH,
ALEX. P. ANKENY

CORRESPONDENCE.

Office Superintendent Indian Affairs,
Salem, Oregon, February 17, 1873.

Messrs. Ankeny, Scott, Goldsmith and Crandall:

Gentlemen: Your note of the 12th instant is received. Prompted by the same motives expressed by you, I furnish herewith a brief statement of the origin and cause of the Modoc war, together with copies of official documents pertaining to that subject:

The Modoc war has become a matter of vast importance and serious concern. Blood has been spilled, and treasure is being consumed in the effort to compel obedience on the part of the desperate band under captain Jack, hold them to their treaty stipulations with the government, and secure peace and safety to settlers on our southern border.

With reference to, and for the benefit of, the sensational press of the country — especially that of California — the Modoc trouble was most opportune. The peaceable arbitration and solution of foreign questions, and the political calm which followed the excitement connected with the presidential contest, had left the newspapers of the land almost without material to work upon, when the first gun of hostilities on Lost river sounded the key note of war, broke the monotonious quiet of the times, and echoed and reverberated throughout the country, until the sound was heard in every nook and corner of the nation. It was necessary to "write up" the subject with electric facility, and a thousand graphic prodigies attacked it on the instant with all the recklessness of ignorance, and a fervor of imagination unrestrained by honesty and inflexible fact. Half forgotten orations of Logan and Red Jacket, and the exploits of Tecumseh — pride and strength of the school boy — have been restored to memory, and launched again at the heads and hearts of the people. The atmosphere becomes lurid with Indian romance, and oroide humanitarians keep up the wail for a weekly stipend about the abuses, frauds, and injustice of the authorities against this band of Modocs.

Many papers, outside of this State, particularly those of a metaphorical tendency, have manufactured and inaugurated Modoc difficulties of their own, and are keeping them up with daily rations of hot condiments from their combustible fancies.

The whole subject, especially the comments upon, and the alleged causes of the war, and the character of the belligerent Indians, has now more and worse distorted faces than a Hindoo god. So many different versions have been given that it would seem that no one who has read them all could possibly fail to be confounded and befogged, so much as to be utterly unable to form any idea of the true cause of the hostilities.

The press of enlightened Oregon, however, having a more definite comprehension of the facts, has almost, without exception, presented them fairly, and it is, therefore, to a certain order of journals in California, which, through prejudice for everything in Oregon, wrong information, indifference or recklessness, whose publications are re-echoed by other papers in the east, that we may attribute the flood of misrepresentation, which has poured over the country to the amazement of those who are in possession of the truth, and the confusion of distant and uninformed communities.

In view of these things, it is due to the cause of truth, and to the people of Oregon, both of which are entitled to the respect even of brilliant newspaper correspondents and reporters, to furnish for publication a brief history, composed mainly of official documents on that subject, in order to dissipate the cloudy fancies of romancists, which have probably served their time, and give the public an understanding of the Modoc question, so simple when the facts are understood.

On the 14th day of October, 1864, a treaty was made and concluded at Klamath Lake, Oregon, between J. W. P. Huntington and William Logan, commissioners, on the part of the United States, and the chiefs and head men of the Klamath and Modoc tribes of Indians, by the terms of which said tribes ceded to the United States all their right, title, interest and claim in and to all lands outside the limits of what is known as Klamath Reservation, which was reserved and set aside for their sole use and occupation, and upon which, by the terms of the treaty, they agreed to go and reside and not depart therefrom, except by permission of the agent or superintendent; and it was further stipulated and agreed that they should demean themselves properly in all respects, and ever thereafter maintain peaceable relations with the whites. One of the Indians who signed the treaty was captain Jack (Indian name, Keint Poos). A gentleman, who was a witness to the treaty, says that captain Jack at first hesitated to assent to its terms, but finally did so with as much apparent willingness as any one. This treaty was amended and ratified by the senate of the United States, July 2, 1866, and the amendments were assented to by captain Jack and the other chiefs and head men of the Modocs, on the 10th day of December, 1869, about which time captain Jack's band went upon the reservation, but becoming dissatisfied, they left some time in February, 1870, and have not since been back, though repeated efforts have been made to persuade them to return. The right of the Indians to the lands on Lost river and Tule Lake being extinguished, that portion of the State was soon settled by whites. When the Indians left the reservation in 1870, they located in the midst of this settlement and remained there until the commencement of the present trouble. In July, 1871, late superintendent Meacham had a sort of understanding with these Indians, to the effect that they should be allowed to remain where they were until he could see whether the government would not give them a new reservation on Lost river. On account of this arrangement, general Canby declined to furnish troops to remove them forcibly when requested to do so by Mr. Meacham, on the 25th of January, 1872. Mr. Meacham's answer to this objection, in his letter of February 8, 1872, says: " They have not kept their part of the agreement, and hence have forfeited any claim they might have had to forbearance."

Persons familiar with the history of captain Jack, say that his first disaffection became manifest when late superintendent Huntington refused to recognize him as head chief of all the Modocs. He claimed that he was mistreated when on the reservation in 1869-70, and when he left took with him all the more venturesome warriors of the tribe, and attempted to set up an independent colony of his own on Lost river. Repeated efforts were made to induce him to return, but he would not. Each successive attempt to persuade him to go only increased his defiance and insolence. Threats and promises had been made, and not executed until he seemed to think the government would allow him to dictate the terms which should settle a difficulty of his own making. It may not be out of place here to say that the "jaw-bone" policy is, in my estimation, the source of more trouble with Indians than anything else. Too much "pow-wow" is the prime cause of the trouble with captain Jack, who has a remarkable faculty of misconstruing everything said to suit his own purposes, and then claiming that bad faith has been practiced. A little prompt action and less talk, when he first left the reservation, before he had become emboldened by repeated successes in "pow-wowing," would have accomplished the desired object, and the Modoc war would not have been.

The present humane policy of the government toward Indians, I believe to be the best ever adopted. Humanitarian ideas which do not embrace the whole human family are more circumscribed than mine, but experience teaches us that the restraining powers of the government must sometimes be brought into requisition, in order to enforce obedience to law, and induce proper respect to be paid by some to the rights of others. In reporting against the propriety of locating captain Jack's band elsewhere than on Klamath Reservation, I was governed by the recommendations of Messrs. Dyar, I. D. Applegate, colonel Otis and late superintendent Meacham, as well as the fact that the people who had settled on Tule Lake and Lost river had vested rights in the land, of which these Indians had divested themselves by the treaty, and that it would be a violation of equity and justice to locate them in their midst, and the only new location desired by them was in this vicinity. I believed further, that to yield thus to this whim of captain Jack, would only pave the way to future concessions whenever he should deem himself aggrieved, or become dissatisfied with the restraints of a reservation.

The whole matter may be summed up in a few words: These Indians made a treaty, agreed to go to Klamath Reservation, which they accepted in lieu of all other lands to which they had ever before set up any claim, to remain thereon, and not depart therefrom without first obtaining leave of the agent or superintendent, and to maintain peaceable relations with all people. The country they thus relinquished all right to was settled by the whites under the homestead and pre-emption laws of the United States. Improper advice was given captain Jack by white men of California; he left the reservation without leave, returned to the country he had given up, and persisted in claiming and living upon it ; levying black mail upon the settlers, taking their property, insulting their families, and threatening their lives. Numerous letters and petitions went to Washington, and thereupon the government ordered that they be removed to the reservation, forcibly if necessary. They refused to go, fired upon the troops —our soldiers returned the fire, and thus the war commenced. They are the only belligerently inclined Indians in Oregon, and unless such terms shall be made with this band as will convey the idea of a victory on the part of captain Jack, we may look for no more Indian outbreaks.

Let captain Jack dictate his own terms, and it may not be long before the Klamaths, the Snakes, some of the Umatillas, and others may feign to be aggrieved, and follow Jack's precedent. Viewing the whole situation, and considering the importance of adjusting and determining the difficulties in a proper way, and for the best interests of whites and Indians, I believed that they should be required to surrender unconditionally, lay down their arms and go to the reservation, and that the murderers of citizens should be turned over to the civil authorities to be dealt with according to law, and I so reported.

Very respectfully,

Your obedient servant,

(Signed) **T. B. ODENEAL,**
Superintendent Indian Affairs, Oregon.

[COPY]

Hon. A. B. MEACHAM,
Superintendent Indian Affairs.

General CANBY,
Commanding Department Columbia.

We, the undersigned citizens of Lost and Link river, Klamath and Tule Lake country, after suffering years of annoyance from the presence of the Modoc Indians, through the delay of the Indian and military department, have not been removed to the reservation, as required by the treaty stipulations of 1864, entered into by the authorized agents of the government and the chiefs of the Modoc Indians, by which all their lands were ceded to the United States, except those embraced in the reservation, as stipulated in said treaty. But, notwithstanding all the conditions of said treaty have been faithfully performed, on the part of the government, it is a well known fact that a factious band of the Modocs, of about three hundred, who were parties to that treaty, have, through the influence of citizens of an adjoining State — who have been engaged in an illicit traffic with them — have been instigated to set the authority of the government at defiance, and to utterly refuse compliance with their treaty stipulations by going on the reservation; and since there is no longer any conflict between the Indians and military department, such as prevented sub-agent Applegate from bringing those Indians on the reservation, we, therefore, make this earnest appeal to you for relief, knowing that you have the cavalry force. We petitioned to be sent to Fort Klamath two years ago for this specific purpose, at your command. We ask you to use it for the purpose it was procured for, that the departments, both civil and military, have not been kept ignorant of the fact that we have been repeatedly on the verge of a desolating Indian war with this band of outlaws, who, by your delay to enforce the treaty, have been led to despise, rather than respect the authority of the government.

Their long continued success in defying its authorites has emboldened them in their defiant and hostile bearing, until further forbearance on our part would cease to be a virtue; that, in many instances, our families have become alarmed at their threats to kill and burn, until we were compelled to remove them for safety across the Cascade mountains, thereby suffering great loss of time and property; that the agents at Klamath and commissary at Yainax, during this long delay, growing out of this unfortunate conflict of departments, have done all they could to prevent a war, and bring about an amicable adjustment of our troubles we have no reason to doubt; but we ask now, since no such conflict exists, shall a petty Indian chief, with twenty desperadoes, and a squallid band of three hundred miserable savages, any longer set at defiance the strong arm of the government, driving our citizens from their homes, threatening their lives, and destroying our property?

Their removal to the reservation, in the winter season, may be easily accomplished by any one acquainted with them and their country, and will not require more force than could be furnished from Fort Klamath to do it. We recommended commissary I. D. Applegate, of Yainax, to the consideration of the department, as a suitable man to take charge of any force or expedition looking to their removal. His long connection with the Indian department, and thorough knowledge of them and their country, and all the facts connected with this whole Modoc question, and as a stock-raiser equally interested with us in their removal, point him out to us as the right man in the right place in charge of this much needed expedition for the removal of this band of Modocs to their reservation, for which your petitioners will ever pray.

I. N. Shook,
Samuel Colver,
James H. Calahan,
David P. Shook,
J. J. Bratton,
Paul Bratton,
H. Duncan,
C. Rilgone,
Joseph Langell,
Simpson Wilson,
Thomas Wilson,
Frank Hifling,
James Vinson,
G. S. Miller,
Edwin Crook,
A. C. Modie,
O. H. Swingle,
C. A. Miller,
J. C. Turnidge,
G. B. Vanresser,
J. H. Springer,
J. V. Rubru,
H. Bailmauk,

Thomas Collar,
J. M. Rambo,
D. Davis,
W. Dingman,
John Clean,
W. H. Miller,
Willis Hall,
E. Hall,
A. Hall,
J. T. Aront,
Joseph Seeds,
John E. Naylor,
George Nurse,
Edward Overton,
William Roberts,
‘ John Gotbrood,
W. Hicks,
O. A. Stearns,
O. L. Stearns,
John Fulkerson,
Isaac Harris,
George Thomas.

Another petition addressed to Governor Grover, and signed by sixty-five citizens of Lost river, Klamath and Tule Lake country, asks for protection, and among other things says:

"Our reasons for this request are these: We have been harrassed and bothered for the last four years by this renegade band of lawless Modoc Indians. They are extremely saucy and menacing in their repeated threats against settlers and their stock; they set up a claim to our homes; they frequently draw guns an pistols on inoffensive citizens; they recently fired at the house of citizen Ball; they watch the men leave their houses, and then go to the house and insult the female inmates of our sacred homes; they boast defiance to the authorities, etc."

Upon the receipt of these petitions, honorable A. B. Meacham, then superintendent of Indian affairs, addressed the following letter to the commander of the department of the Columbia:

OFFICE SUPERINTENDENT INDIAN AFFAIRS,
Salem, Oregon, January 25, 1872.

SIR: Enclosed please find a petition from citizens of Jackson county, Oregon, for removal of Modoc Indians. I would respectfully ask that the said Indians be removed to Yainax Station on Klamath Reservation, by the military force now at Fort Klamath. I would also suggest that sufficient force be sent on this mission to insure success, say fifty men. I have ordered arrangements to subsist the

Modocs at the place above named, and have instructed I. D. Applegate, commissary at Yainax, to confer with commander at post, and accompany said expedition if agreeable to your department. Now, if it is not consistent with your views on the subject to comply with the above request, I would respectfully ask that a military force of the number designated be placed, subject to requisition of commissary Applegate, for the purpose above stated. Winter is the only time to successfully operate against these Indians.

I regret very much the necessity of this action, but the peace and welfare of white settlers and Indians demand that it be done promptly.

Very respectfully,

Your obedient servant,

(Signed)　　　　　　A. B. MEACHAM,

Supt. Indian Affairs in Oregon.

General E. R. S. CANBY,

Commanding Dep. of Columbia, Portland, Oregon.

HEADQUARTERS DEPARTMENT OF THE COLUMBIA,
Portland, Oregon, February 5, 1872.

HON. A. B. MEACHAM,
Supt. Indian Affairs for Oregon, Salem, Oregon.

SIR: I have the honor to acknowledge the receipt of your communication of January 25th, in relation to the Modoc Indians, and also of the sketch of the Klamath Reservation, as recently surveyed, which reached me on Saturday. Referring to the report of the commissioners, appointed by you to confer with the Modoc chiefs, and transmitted in your letter of August 28, 1871, I find it stated that as the result of that conference, "under the circumstances, we did not think it advisable to talk very much with them, further than to advise them not to do any thing that would have a tendency to cause any collision between them and the settlers, *to remain where they were until they saw you,* not to resist the military under any circumstances, and to pay no attention to the talk of irresponsible parties." This has been understood as a temporary settlement of the question, and as authorizing them to remain for that time at the point where they were found by the commissioners, unless some different arrangement has since been made. I think that it would not be expedient, or politic, to send a military force against these Indians, or, at least, until notified of the determination of the government of the point at which they are to be established, and fully warned that they will be treated as enemies if within a reasonable and specified time they do not establish themselves as required. I shall be pleased to hear from you fully upon this subject, and as early as may be convenient, and in the meantime will send a copy of your communication to the commanding officer at Fort Klamath, to take all necessary measures to protect the settlers against hostilities from the Modocs, and to prepare to aid in their removal to the point indicated in your communication, should forcible means become necessary.

Very respectfully,

Your obedient servant,

(Signed)   ED. W. R. CANBY,
Brigadier General Commanding.

[A true copy.]

———

OFFICE SUPERINTENDENT INDIAN AFFAIRS,

Salem. Oregon, February 8, 1872.

SIR: I have the honor to acknowledge the receipt of your letter of the fifth instant. In reply, in part, submit herewith copy of letter to commissioner on this subject; further, would state that I had in my annual report, for 1871. recommended that a small reservation be made for the Modoc Indians at the north end of Modoc Lake. No action has been had by the department that I am aware of.

My reasons for asking assistance are set forth, or rather suggested, by the petition forwarded to you, otherwise I would have deferred action until such time as instructions might be forwarded from Washington city. Since my letter to you, I have received a communication from Hon. Jesse Applegate on this Modoc question, a copy of which please find enclosed herewith. I have also learned from I. D. Applegate, commissary in charge of Yainax, and from J. N. High, Indian sub-agent at Klamath, that hostilities were imminent. I am of the opinion that any attempt to arrest the chief and his " body guard" will be resisted by them, and serious consequences may result. Nevertheless the white settlers must be protected.

In your letter you refer to the agreement made with commissioners sent by this department last July, and suggested that no action be had until they were notified to place themselves upon the reservation, etc. That council was held at Clear Lake, some sixty miles southeast of Modoc Lake, where they are now located, hence you perceive they have not kept their part of the agreement, and have forfeited any claim they might have had to forbearance.

I do not realize that there is any unjustifiable breach of our part of the compact of July last, by compelling them to go on the reservation. Had they behaved honestly, and on their part maintained peaceable relations with the white settlers, they might have remained at Modoc Lake undisturbed. Such has not been the case, and much as I regret the necessity for forcible arrest and return to the reservation, I can see no other way to secure peace and mete out justice.

I would respectfully recommend that the commander at Fort Klamath be instructed to arrest the chief and five or six of the head men, and hold them in confinement until some further orders shall have been received from department at Washington city.

Very respectfully,

Your obedient servant,

(Signed) A. B. MEACHAM,

Supt. Indian Affairs in Oregon.

General ED. CANBY,

Commanding Dept. of Columbia, Portland Oregon.

[COPY]

OFFICE SUPERINTENDENT INDIAN AFFAIRS,

Salem Oregon, February 19, 1872.

SIR: Governor Grover has this day called on me, and is very solicitious about Modoc matters. I have no further information, but from private letters learn that the white settlers are making preparations for self defense. I can only renew my recommendation that the Modoc chief and his head men be placed under arrest at Fort Klamath.

Very respectfully,

Your obedient servant,

(Signed)   A. B. MEACHAM,

Supt. Indian Affairs in Oregon.

General E. R. S. CANBY,

Commanding, etc., Portland.

On the 11th day of April last colonel Elmer Otis and late superintendent Meacham were in the office of the superintendent of Indian affairs, at Salem, and, at the request of the present superintendent, they expressed their views, in writing, in regard to the Modocs and other Indians, as follows:

Salem, Oregon, April 11, 1872.

T. B. ODENEAL,

Superintendent Indian Affairs.

SIR: At your request I put the following recommendations in writing:

I would recommend that the permission for captain Jack's band of Modocs to remain where they now are until the question of a new reservation be decided in the vicinity of Tule Lake, given by Mr. Meacham, be withdrawn, and that they be directed to go on the Klamath Reservation, as per treaty of October, 1864. That this order be given some time in the latter part of September, so that in case they refused, the military authorities could put them upon the reservation the following winter — the best time for "corraling" them, should they prove refractory — that at least two of their leaders, captain Jack and Black Jim, be removed from them and sent to Siletz, or any other place you might suggest.   *   *   *   *

The reasons why I make this recommendation, with reference to the Modocs, is, that where they are now they are very insolent, insulting to families, and the settlers are generally of the opinion that they are dangerous to both life and property. I do not believe they will live where they now are in peace with the whites any length of time, without the presence of a military force sufficiently large to make them behave themselves. There is now a force of fifty men and three officers in their immediate country.

I would propose and strongly recommend, that We-ah-was' band, Oche-hoes' band, the band at McDermit, and the band on the Truckee Reservation, or Pyramid Lake Reservation (official name of the reservation not known by me), be brought on a reservation on the head waters of the Malheur, or Stein's mountain country.

I make the above recommendations, after commanding the military districts of Nevada, Owyhee, and district of the Lakes, successively since December of 1867.

Very respectfully,

Your obedient servant,

(Signed)   ELMER OTIS,

Major First Cavalry
Commanding District of the Lakes.

Salem, Oregon, April 11, 1872.

Major ELMER OTIS,

   Commanding District of the Lakes,

SIR: I have been relieved by my successor, Hon. T. B. Odeneal, notwithstanding which, however, I still feel an abiding interest in whatever pertains to the welfare of the country and Indians, and do not hesitate to say that your suggestions meet the case exactly, as I understand the case to be to select a reservation either on the Malheur or Stein mountain country, and to consoldidate thereon the Harney, McDermit, and Ochehos band of Snakes, and to consolidate and locate the Modocs, with the Wal-pah-pe, at Yainax, thus securing peace to the Modoc country.

Very respectfully,

      Your obedient servant,

(Signed)   **A. B. MEACHAM,**
                  Late Supt. Indian Affairs.

In his report to General Canby, bearing date April 15, 1872, Colonel Elmer Otis, commander of district of the Lakes, says:

"They (the Modocs) signed a treaty in October, 1864, to go on the Klamath Reservation. They came on the reservation in the Fall of 1869. A portion of them, with the old chief, still remain, but captain Jack, who signed the treaty in 1864, became dissatisfied soon after coming on the reservation, and in February, 1870, formed a band, numbering now probably sixty warriors, and left the reservation. going to Lost river and Tule Lake. Last fall. superintendent Meacham promised to allow them to remain where they are until he could see if a small reservation could not be set aside for them on the north end of Tule Lake. These Indians are still in this country, and are insolent and insulting in many instances to the white settlers, and the latter generally deem this band of Modocs unsafe to both life and property. If a military force was present they could probably be removed peaceably to camp Yainax, on Klamath Reservation, and by moving the Piutes now there, would leave them homes and farms for their cultivation. I am of the opinion that if left where they now are, it will probably lead to serious outbreak in time."

—

DEPARTMENT OF THE INTERIOR.

Office of Indian Affairs,
Washington. D. C, April 12. 1872.

SIR: I enclose herewith copies of papers received by this department by reference from the honorable secretary of war, in reference to the hostile attitude of, and apprehended trouble with, the Modoc tribe of Indians.

You are instructed to have the Modoc Indians removed, if practicable, to the reservation set apart for them under the treaty concluded with said Indians, October 14, 1864, and, if removed, to see that they are properly protected from the Klamath Indians.

If they can not be removed to or kept on the reservation, you will report your views as to the practicability of locating them at some other point, and if favorable to such location, you will give a description by natural boundaries, if no other can be given, of the reservation that should be set aside for them.

Very respectfully,

Your obedient servant,

F. A. WALKER,
Commissioner.

T. B. ODENEAL, Esq.,
Superintendent Indian Affairs, Salem, Oregon.

It being impracticable for the present superintendent to go in person to the Klamath country, he referred the execution of the foregoing order to L. S. Dyar, United States Indian agent at Klamath agency, and Ivon D. Applegate, commissary in charge of camp Yainax, on Klamath Reservation; and, on the 16th of May, 1872, they reported that on the 14th of the same month they met the chiefs and head men of the Modocs, both those on and off the reservation, at the military camp on Lost river; that they used every argument to induce them to return peaceably to the reservation, telling them that this was the desire of the department; that such action would insure them all the rights and priviliges now enjoyed by the other Indians on the reservation, and that they should be fully protected against any injustice the Klamaths might be disposed to do them. Captain Jack made substantially the following speech:

"We are good people, and will not kill or frighten anybody. We want peace and friendship. I am well known and understood by the people of Yreka, California, and am governed by their advice. I do not want to live upon the reservation, for the Indians there are poorly clothed, suffer from hunger, and even have to leave the reservation sometimes to make a living. We are willing to have whites live in our country, but do not want them to locate on the west side and near the mouth of Lost river, where we have our winter camps. The settlers are continually lying about my people and trying to make trouble."

They would not go upon the reservation. In regard to selecting a new reservation for them, Messrs. Dyar and Applegate say:

"The Modocs, as parties to the treaty of 1864, ceded to the United States the very country over which they are now roving. Their right being thus extinguished, the country was thrown open to settlement; much of it has been located as State land, and nearly every foot fit for cultivation has been taken up by settlers, whose thousands of horses, cattle and sheep are ranging over it. The country where these Modocs are is a pastoral region, not an agricultural country, and to undertake to maintain them on a small reservation there would probably cost more than to furnish for them and the Klamath's on Klamath Reservation, which is so well fitted by its various resources as a home for them. The white settlers are very much opposed to establishing a new reservation for this band, and their determined opposition would keep up a continual conflict. "

The papers from the honorable secretary of war, referred to by the honorable commissioner of Indian affairs, in his letter of April 12, 1872, consisted of a petition of settlers and letters written by honorable Jesse Applegate, general Canby, governor Grover, late superintendent Meacham, colonel Otis, and other gentlemen. After a careful examination of all these papers, as well as the report of agent Dyar and commissary Applegate, the superintendent addressed the following letter to the commissioner of Indian affairs:

OFFICE SUPERINTENDENT INDIAN AFFAIRS,

Salem, Oregon, June 17, 1872.

SIR: In answer to your letter of the 12th of April last, enclosing copies of papers from the honorable secretary of war, in reference to the hostile attitude of, and apprehended trouble with, the Modoc Indians, I have the honor to report that, in pursuance of your instructions therein contained, I at once directed agent Dyar, of Klamath agency, and Ivon D. Applegate, commissary in charge of camp Yainax, to meet the chiefs and head men of said tribe of Indians, and endeavor to persuade them to go upon the Klamath Reservation, authorizing the assurance to be given that they should be fully protected.

"A counsel was held with said Indians on the 14th ultimo, and the result thereof is contained in the report of Mr. Applegate [approved by Mr. Dyar], a copy of which is herewith enclosed. I referred the matter to the gentlemen named, for the reason that Mr. Applegate has for many years been intimately acquainted with these Indians, speaks their language, and possesses their confidence to an extent equal to any one else. [See indorsement of Mr. Applegate by the settlers in that country, in the petition herewith published.]

"The leaders of these Indians are desperadoes — brave, daring and reckless — and their superior sagacity enables them to exercise full and complete control over the rest of the tribe. They have for so long a time been permitted to do as they please, that they imagine they are too powerful to be controlled by the government, and that they can, with impunity, defy its authority. This, in my opinion, is the whole secret of their insubordination. They must, in some way, be convinced of their error in this respect, by such firm, decided action, as will leave no doubt in their minds in regard to the fact that we intend that they must be obedient to law and faithful to their treaty obligations. This need not, and with proper management, will not, I think, require the use of force. When they shall have been thus convinced, we can with reasonable hope of success, commence the work of civilizing and transforming them from their present savage state into peaceable, self-controlling and self-supporting men and women.

" Unless the leaders shall in some way be restrained from pursuing the reckless, defiant course they have heretofore been permitted to pursue, all theories in regard to their advancement in civilization must fail. As well might we expect our own youth to practice christian virtues under the tutorship of the ' bandits of the Osage,' or the 'road agents' of Montana, as to think of instilling any good into the minds of the Modocs while under the exclusive control of their present leaders.

"I think the most effectual way to bring about a peaceable solution of the troubles, is to take the head men into custody, and hold them at some point remote from their tribe until they shall agree to behave themselvess. We deprive white men of their liberty as a reformatory measure, and it could not be less humane to pursue the same course toward these chiefs.

"Not long since I had a conversation with major Elmer Otis, who was in command of the troops in the district, including these Indians, in which he expressed the opinion that all trouble with them conld be settled by arresting the leaders, and compelling the others to go upon Klamath Reservation ; but it was his opinion that positive orders should not be given to this effect until about the last of September, so that in case of refusal the military could compel obedience. His opinion, as well as that of Messrs. Applegate and Dyar, and all others from whom I have obtained any information, is that camp Yainax, on Klamath Reservation, is the best place in that whole country for the Modocs ; that they will be as well contented, and as easily kept there as at any other place that could be selected, and I agree with them, and, therefore respectfully report against the propriety of locating them elsewhere."

Very respectfully,

Your obedient servant,

(Signed) T. B. ODENEAL,

Superintendent Indian Affairs, Oregon.

Hon. F. A. WALKER,

Commissioner, etc., Washington, D. C.

DEPARTMENT OF THE INTERIOR,

Office of Indian Affairs,

Washington, D. C., July 6, 1872.

SIR: I have received your report, dated the 17th ultimo, enclosing copies of letters from I. D. Applegate, dated the 8th and 16th of May last, in reply to a communication from this office, dated April 12, 1872, relative to the removal of the Modoc Indians to the Klamath Reservation, or the propriety of having a new reservation set apart for them.

In your report you state that it is the opinion of major Elmer Otis, as well as that of Messrs. Applegate and Dyar, that camp Yainax, on Klamath Reservation, is the best place in that whole country for the Modoc Indians; that they will be as well contented and as easily kept there, as at any other place that could be selected, and you agree with them in their opinion and report against the propriety of locating them elsewhere.

You further state that the leaders of the Modoc Indians are desperadoes — brave, daring and reckless — and defy the authority of the government with impunity, and that it will be necessary to arrest these leaders and convince them of their error before any civilizing influences can be brought to bear upon the tribe.

Your recommendations, so far as the Modoc Indians are concerned, are approved, and you are directed to remove them to the Klamath Reservation peaceably if you can, but forcibly if you must, at the time suggested in your report.

You will exercise your discretion about making arrests of the leaders, avoiding any unnecessary violence or resort to extreme measures.

Very respectfully,

Your obedient servant,

F. A. WALKER,
Commissioner.

T. B. ODENEAL, Esq.,
Superintendent Indian Affairs, Salem, Oregon.

[COPY]

OFFICE SUPERINTENDENT INDIAN AFFAIRS,

Salem, Oregon, December 23, 1872.

SIR: In your letter of the 6th of July last you directed me to remove the Modoc Indians to Klamath Reservation, peaceably if I could, but forciby if I must.

For the purpose of executing this order, I left here on the 20th of November, and arrived at Klamath agency on the 25th of the same month. Learning that captain Jack's band of Modocs was then camped on Lost river, I immediately dispatched messenger James Brown and I. D. Applegate to said camp with the following message:

"Say to them that I wish to meet the head men at Link river, on the 27th instant, and to talk with them. Impress upon them the importance of meeting me. Tell them that I entertain none but the most friendly feelings for them, and that the object of the interview sought is to advance their interests and promote their welfare. That I have made ample provisions for their comfortable subsistance at camp Yainax, on Klamath Reservation; and desire to have them go there and receive their proportion of the annuities ; that if they will go with you to the reservation within a reasonable time — as soon as they can get ready — they shall be fairly and justly dealt with, and fully protected in all their rights against any injustice which other tribes might be disposed to do them. If they agree to go with you, say to them that they need not meet me as requested, and that I will see them at Yainax. In the event they decline to go to the reservation, you will say they must meet me at Link river, as I desire to and must come to a positive understanding with them. "

On the same day I addressed the following letter to lieutenant colonel Wheaton, commanding the district of the lakes, to wit:

OREGON SUPERINTENDENCY,
Klamath Agency, November 25, 1872.

SIR: I am here for the purpose of putting the Modoc Indians upon this reservation, in pursuance of an order from the honorable commissioner of Indian affairs, a copy of which is as follows: "You are directed to remove the Modoc Indians to Klamath Reservation, peaceably if you can, but forcibly if you must."

I have requested the head men of the tribe to meet me at Link river on the 27th instant, at which time I shall endeavor to persuade them to return to the reservation. If they shall refuse to come voluntarily, then I shall call upon you for a force sufficient to compel them to do so. They have some eighty well armed warriors, and I would suggest that as large a force be brought to bear against them at once as you can conveniently furnish, in the event it shall be determined that they cannot be removed peaceably.

Immediately after the conference referred to I will inform you of the result thereof, and in the meantime I have to request that all necessary preliminary arrangements be made for concentrating the forces at your command, and having them ready for active operations.

Very respectfully,

Your obedient servant,

(Signed)   T. B. ODENEAL,
Superintendent Indian Affairs, Oregon.

Lieutenant Colonel FRANK WHEATON,
Commanding District of the Lakes,
Camp Warner, Oregon.

My plan was, if they could not be removed peaceably, to bring so large a force against them as to overawe them at once, and thus insure the execution of the order without fighting.

Lost river is fifty-five miles from Klamath agency — twenty three miles from Link river. On the day appointed, in company with agent L. S. Dyer, I went to the place designated for the meeting, and there met the messengers, who reported that they had been to the camp of captain Jack's band of Modocs, and had informed the head men of everything contained in my instructions, and besides had used every argument in their power to persuade them to meet me, or go upon the reservation. That they peremptorily declined to do either. Captain Jack, the head chief, made sudstantially the following speech:

"Say to the superintendent that we do not wish to see him, or to talk with him. We do not want any white man to tell us what to do. Our friends and counsellors are men in Yreka, California. They tell us to stay where we are, and we intend to do it, and will not go upon the reservation. I am tired of being talked to, and am done with talking."

After considering and discussing the matter with agent Dyar and Mr. Applegate, and receiving from them the positive opinion that nothing but the appearance of an armed force at their camp could have any influence whatever upon them, I concluded to call for such force, and accordingly sent Mr. Applegate to Fort Klamath with the following letter, which

I authorized him to deliver to major John Green, commanding that post, and that if. he had not sufficient authority and force to act, to forward the same to colonel Wheaton, to wit:

 OREGON SUPERINTENDENCY,

Link River, November 27, 1872.

SIR: The bearer of this, captain I. D. Applegate, has just returned from the camp of the Modoc Indians, and he informs me that they defiantly decline to meet me at this place, in accordance with my request sent by him. They authorized him to say that they did not desire to see or to talk with me, and that they would not go upon Klamath Reservation. In order, therefore, to carry out the instructions of the honorable commissiener of Indian affairs, I have to request that you furnish a sufficient force to compel said Indians to go to camp Yainax, on Klamath Reservation.

I transfer the whole matter to your department, without assuming to dictate the course you shall pursue in executing the order aforesaid, trusting, however, that you may accomplish the object desired without the shedding of blood, if possible to avoid it.

If it shall become necessary to use force, then I have to request that you arrest captain Jack, Black Jim, and Scar-faced Charley, and hold them in custody, subject to my orders.

I am informed that these leaders, with only about half of their warriors, are camped near the mouth of Lost river, and if the force could be immediately sent to that place I think they might be induced to surrender and come upon the reservation without further trouble. "

Very respectfully,

Your obedient servant,

(Signed)   T. B. ODENEAL,

Superintendent Indian Affairs, Oregon.

This letter was addressed to no one on the inside, but was sent to major Green, with instructions to the bearer, Mr. Applegate, to address it to colonel Frank Wheaton, camp Warner, in the event major Green had not authority and force sufficient to enable him to act. He had told me on the 26th that he had orders to act, but I did not learn to what extent. I am informed that my letter was immediately forwarded to colonel Wheaton.

On the 28th of November, at five o'clock, P. M., a special messenger delivered to me a letter from major Green, a copy of which is as follows:

" HEADQUARTERS, FORT KLAMATH,
" *November 28, 1872.*

" Mr. T. B. ODENEAL,
"*Superintendent Indian Affairs.*

" SIR: In compliance with your written request of yesterday, I will state that captain Jackson will leave this post about noon to-day, with about thirty men ; will be at Link river to-night, and I hope before morning at captain Jack's camp.

" I am, sir, very respectfully,

" Your obedient servant,

"JOHN GREEN,
"*Major First Cavalry Commanding Post.*"

The impression seemed prevalent among military men, and some others, that, on account of the weather and other adverse circumstances surrounding the Indians, that they would surrender and go to the reservation as soon as they saw that there was a probability that troops would be used against them, if they should refuse to go.

This force was, in my estimation, too small, and as soon as I received major Green's letter I sent James Brown, messenger in this office, in company with a man named Crawley (who lived within a quarter of a mile of the camp of the Modocs), to notify all settlers, who could be in any danger in the event of an unsuccessful engagement with the Indians, that the cavalry were coming. They notified several families, who went with them to Crawley's house, arriving there at half-past twelve o'clock that night. Mr. Brown says he knew nothing of other settlers living below Crawley's; that there were six men there with him, all well acquainted with the country; that no one said anything about there being other settlers who might be in danger. Mr. Brown also says that all could have been notified easily before daylight. If this had been done, no one would have been murdered. I state facts only. Feeling conscious that I did everything in my power to avert all danger, and knowing that blaming others can not bring the dead to life, or relieve the anguish of sorrowing friends, I shall offer no words of censure against any one for the sad results.

Learning that the troops would not come by way of Link river (where I was), I, at one o'clock in the morning of the 29th, went to a point on the road which they would pass, some three miles distant, and there gave captain Jackson, at his request, verbal directions substantially as follows:

"When you arrive at the camp of the Modocs, request an interview with the head men, and say to them that you did not come to fight or to harm them, but to have them go peaceably to camp Yainax, on Klamath Reservation, where ample provision has been made for their comfortable subsistence, and where by their treaty they agreed to live. Talk kindly but firmly to them, and whatever else you may do, I desire to urge that if there is any fighting, let the Indians be the aggressors ; fire not a gun, except in self-defence, after they have first fired upon you."

The troops arrived at the camp of the Modocs at seven o'clock in the morning, obtained an interview, and a conversation ensued, lasting some three quarters of an hour. Captain Jackson has since informed me that he repeated to them all I requested him to say, and used every argument he could to induce them to go. All proving ineffectual, he demanded of them to lay down their arms, when one of the leaders Scar-faced Charley with an oath, said he would shoot one officer, and fired at lieutenant Boutelle, who was in front of his men. A general firing commenced at once on both sides. The battle lasted some two hours, when the Indians escaped, but returned again in the afternoon and attacked the troops.

The murders of citizens were committed by six men and one woman. All can be identified. The matter being in the hands of the military, I have of course exercised no control since the battle, further than to suggest that the Indians should be required to surrender, lay down their arms and go to the reser-vation, and that the murderers be delivered to the civil authorities to be dealt with according to law. I have also suggested that the leaders be taken charge of, and held subject to further orders.

The military purpose pursuing until they capture them. I believe this the only safe way to do. Should the troops return to their posts, the Indians would regard it as a defeat of the government, their insolence and defiance would become still more intolerable, and a general warfare might be waged until every settler in that region would be murdered. Other Indians, now peaceable, seeing their success, would hasten to join them, and the result would be the most gigantic Indian war of modern times. * *

Indians should be dealt with kindly and humanely, but more as if they were children than men, until they can be educated in the ways and habits of civilized life. The government should faithfully perform all its promises, and as a father enforces his rules and mandates, so should they be made to fulfill their promises and argreements. Believing, as I ever have, that many acts of injustice have, in the past, been committed against them by representatives of the government, as well as by individual white men, my sympathies are enlisted in their favor when I see any attempt made to invade or trample upon their rights. I can make due allowance for the ignorance which their habits, condition, and want of opportunity to become enlightened, has entailed upon them. But there are exceptions to all rules. A majority of the Modocs have for years been residing upon the reservation, and demeaning themselves properly, while captain Jack, disregarding the counsel of the head chief, Scon-chin, has persisted in roaming whithersoever he pleased, taking as many others with him as he could persuade to go. No injustice has ever been done these Modocs that I am aware of, though they have been bad Indians in the past, having murdered helpless emigrants passing through their country by the score. Captain Jack and the other leaders of his band are not educated in books, but for natural common sense they are not much inferior to ordinary white men. They are schooled in all the vices of our race, and have no apparent desire for any other kind of knowledge. It is not ignorance which impels them to pursue the course they do. They know better, but not unlike many white men, are destitute of all moral principle, and have no respect for the rights of others. There are enough of them to demoralize all the Indians in that part of the State, and I believe that to subdue them now, is not only the most merciful and christianlike, but the only safe way to deal with them. For eight years they have been permitted to baffle and defy the government in the course desired to be pursued for their benefit, until many Indians on the reservation, familiar with their conduct, were becoming discontented, and soon would have fled from the restraints, as they consider them, connected with living at an agency. The good of all the Indians in that part of the State demanded that your order be executed without further delay. I tried to carry out your instructions peaceably. Persuasive measures proved fruitless. The military tried to effect the object desired, by both argument and intimidation. All failed. The Indians commenced hostilities, and now, I think, no terms should be made with the band

which could interfere with afterwards arresting and removing the leaders, and the trial of the murderers.
❊   ❊   ❊   ❊   ❊   ❊

Since you first ordered these Indians to be removed, I have received many letters from citizens, some addressed to me, and some by reference from the governor, complaining of captain Jack's band, and asking for relief. They were becoming more insolent every day. When they wanted a barrel of flour or a beef, they would go and demand it of the nearest settler, who, being afraid to refuse, gave them whatever they called for. A dozen or more would go into a house, demand their breakfast, dinner, or supper, and the frightened women, not daring to refuse, would prepare the meal for them while they lounged around on the beds, or sat and smoked by the fire. The land had been taken under the homestead and pre-emption laws, yet the Indians claimed it, and would demand hay and grain as rent.

T. B. ODENEAL,
Superintendent Indian Affairs.

Honorable Commissioner Indian Affairs,
Washington, D. C.

Extracts from monthly report of L. S. Dyar, United States Indian agent, for month of November, 1872, to honorable commissioner Indian affairs: *   *

It is well known that the Modocs, by treaty stipulations, belong on this reservation, and were formerly here, and also that some years ago they ran away, and have since constantly refused to return, setting at defiance the authority of the government. It is also understood that the commissioner of Indian affairs, upon the recommendation of colonel Otis, I. D. Applegate, commissary in charge at Yainax, myself, and perhaps superintendent Odeneal, authorized the superintendent to remove captain Jack's band of Modocs to this reservation, "peaceably if he could, forcibly if he must," and the month of October was the time fixed for their removal. But upon advice, of those best acquainted with the "situation," and very wisely too, I think, it was deferred until winter should set in.

On the 25th of November superintendent Odeneal sent Mr. I. D. Applegate, a man intimately acquainted with Indian character, and Mr. James Brown, department messenger, from Linkville to the camp of the Modocs, at the mouth of Lost river, with instructions to see captain Jack, and the leading men, and tell them that the superintendent wished them to meet him at Link river, about twenty miles from their camp, on the 28th, or, if they would not meet him there, to come upon the reservation, and he would see them here; that ample provision had been made for their subsistance and comfort. Mr. Odeneal then came on to the agency, arriving here on the evening of the 25th, and on the 27th I went with him to Link river, to meet the Indians on the 28th, should they consent to come. On the way to Link river we met Mr. Applegate returning from the Modoc camp, and he reported that captain Jack refused to meet Mr. Odeneal at Link river; that he did not wish to see the superintendent; that he had done talking; that he was advised by his friends, white men in Yreka, to stay where he was, and that he would not go on the reservation.

On reaching Linkville, Mr. Odeneal immediately sent a messenger to major Green, at Fort Klamath, with a dispatch stating these facts, and turning the matter over to the military, instructing them to bring captain Jack's band upon the reservation, and to do so peacably if possible, but to *bring them.* Major Green, believing that if taken by surprise they would probably not resist, immediately dispatched captain Jackson with about thirty-five mounted men at noon of the 28th, and by marching all night, a distance of fifty-five miles, the detachment reached the main Modoc camp, about day break the next morning. The surprise was complete. Before the Indians were aware of their approach the soldiers were in their camp. Major Jackson immediately called for captain Jack to come out and talk, telling the Indians at the same time that he did not come to fight them, but he wanted them to "lay down their arms and be quiet," and "they should not be hurt."　　　*　　*　　*

They thus continued talking to the Indians for twenty or thirty minutes, and it seemed that they had not decided to fight, until Scar-faced Charley, a leading desperado, who had meantime gone into his hut and painted his face, and dressed up in war costume, came out with his gun, in defiant manner, and, when ordered by captain Jackson to lay it down, refused. Captain Jackson then ordered lieutenant Boutelle to take four men and disarm him. Charley deliberately raised his gun and fired at the lieutenant, who instantly returned the fire, and then the fight commenced. There were about fifteen or twenty warriors in the camp, and they were soon driven to the brush, where they had the advantage of a cover, but after fighting for some time they were driven away with a loss of four or five killed, rnd several wounded, among whom was Black Jim, one of the leaders. None of the leaders were killed, although it was so reported at first.　　　*　　　*　　　*

During the fight, or immediately after, a party of six Indians started down the lake, murdering the helpless settlers who were entirely ignorant of any movements of the military, and thirteen men and boys were killed. The women were allowed to escape. On learning that the soldiers were moving, Mr. Odeneal dispatched two men to warn these settlers, one of whom lived near the scene of the fight, and was well acquainted with the whole country, but they went no further than his own place, leaving all those below unapprised of danger. This accouuts for the terrible massacre.　　*　　*　　*　　*　　*　　*

Some friendly Indians, who were present while Mr. Odeneal's messengers were talking to the Modocs, state that Scar-faced Charley and some others were in favor of killing the messengers, but captain Jack disapproved of it, saying that Mr. Odeneal might come himself in a few days. Had Mr. Odeneal gone to the camp I have but little doubt he would have been killed.

I think the whole course of the superintendent the wisest that could be adopted.

L. S. DYAR,
United States Indian Agent.

APPENDIX.

—

As a sequel to the above official history, the following statement of the findings of the peace commission is appended:

FAIRCHILD'S, HEADQUARTERS PEACE COMMISSION,
California, *March* 6, 1873.

EDITORS BULLETIN: As the peace commission probably closes its labors at this date, it seems proper to give through you to the public an account of the manner in which it has discharged its duties. While awaiting the tedious delays of negotiation, the reasons for its acts have been embodied in the form of reports to the Indian department; but, as the Hon. A. B. Meacham, Chairman of the commission, will report in person at Washingon, the formal written reports may be dispensed with. These reports were prepared and submitted to the commission (after Judge Roseborough was added to it) and to general Canby for their examination. They were approved without conflicting sentiment, except as regards jurisdiction, general Canby being of opinion that the Indians, surrrendering themselves as prisoners of war, would be exempt from process and trial in either Oregon or California, and that the protection promised them by the commission might be assured to them, if the terms of surrender were approved by the federal government. Judge Roseborough dissents from the legal view of the case, but thinks neither state would assert its rights to punish the murderers, if satisfied they would be removed to some distant point beyond the limits of those states never to return.

I send you two reports, not formally adopted or sent as such to Washington, but as representing the conclusions of the commission, and a brief statement of some of the reasons upon which their conclusions are based. I will, in a few days, send you a third paper, which, in the form of a journal or narrative, will give a history of the negotiations with the Indians up to their close, and consequent dissolution of the commission.

Very respectfully,

JESSE APPLEGATE

HEADQUARTERS MODOC PEACE COMMISSION,
FAIRCHILD'S RANCH, California, *Feb.* 22, 1873.

TO HON. H. R. CLUM,
Acting Commissioner of Indian Affairs, Washington, D. C.

SIR: The undersigned, the special commmission " to inquire into the troubles with the Modoc Indians," have had the subject under consideration, and, promising that it will again return to the subject should further developments make it necessary, would respectfully make a partial report in answer to that part of your instructions embraced in the following words, to wit: "The objects to be attained by the commission are these: First, to ascertain the causes which have led to the difficulties and hostilities between the United States troops and the Modocs."

This, the first part of our duties, being an examination into the events of the past, now beyond change, and being useful only as it will enable us to apply the proper remedies for the future, we have thought it best to make a report of the facts now known to us, so that the department may give us its further instructions in regard to the more important branch of our duties, viz: "To devise the most effective and judicious measures for preventing the continuance of these hostilities, and for the restoration of peace."

The conclusions arrived at in regard to the troubles are,

First, Dissatisfaction of the Indians with the Klamath Reservation as a place of residence, owing mainly to the domination of the Klamath Indians on that agency.

Second, To the assertion of their right to a country which they have conveyed by treaty to the United States (of October, 1864), and which is now occupied by settlers under the preference laws of congress.

Third, To their persistent determination to reside in and roam over, at will, the country once belonging to them, and their refusal to abandon or abate these pretentions, though frequently urged to do so by the Indian department

Fourth, That the Indians, by the assertion of the rights of ownership over the Lost River Basin, and treating as *tenants* the white settlers therein, would inevitably lead to a collision between the races.

Fifth, A collision being emminent, superintendent Odeneal, after exhausting all peaceable means of removing the Indians to the reservation where they had agreed to reside, rightfully and properly turned over the execution of the orders of the Indian department to the military arm of the government.

Sixth, Though the force at the disposal of colonel Green, in command at Fort Klamath, proved inadequate to execute the order of the Indian department at Washington, it is our opinion that, in the prompt action of that officer, was the only hope of effecting the arrest of the contumacious Indians; for, by the necessary delay and unavoidable publicity of collecting the disposable forces at the neighboring posts, opportunity would have been given for the Indians to be informed of the intended movement, and its purpose defeated by their withdrawal to their inaccessable fastnesses in the rocks.

The facts upon which the foregoing conclusions are based are briefly as follows:

Though the Klamath and Modoc countries adjoin, the tribes speak the same language and doubtless have a common origin. Bitter feuds have existed and still exist between them. The Klamath Reservation is located exclusively in the Klamath country. To remove the Modocs to it was a measure repugnant to both people, and was probably a mistake — certainly the most difficult article to negotiate in the treaty with the Modocs. It further seems, from the facts, that the Klamath being the stronger tribe, though committing no serious depredations upon their ancient enemies, were arrogant and sometimes oppressive; at least enough so to make the stay of the Modocs at the same agency very uncomfortable, and since the Yainax station was established on the same Reservation, forty-five miles eastward of the Klamath agency, the chief, Schon-chin,. and the other Modocs faithful to the stipulations of the treaty of October, 1864, have, at their request, resided at that station.

Beside the wrongs inflicted upon them by the Klamaths, captain Jack and his band have complained of ill-treatment from the agents in charge at Klamath. If this complaint be well founded, we are satisfied that the fault lies in the stipulations of the treaty, not in their execution by the agents and employees of the department. If insufficient, the distributions of food and clothing have been impartial. No indulgencies have been allowed to one tribe or band of Indians not extended in equal terms to all; and while the Klamaths, Snakes and Schon-chin's band of Modocs have been content, or at least have borne their grievances with patience, captian Jack and his followers alone have found cause to justify a refusal to perform their treaty stipulations and deny their binding force upon them.

From the denial of the binding force of the treaty of October 14, 1864, by the Modocs, has grown all the difficulties, troubles, and lastly bloodshed, between the whites and these savages. Mistaking the mercy and forbearance of the government for a baser passion, these people, from long impunity, have become continually more bold and aggressive; and to the credit of the settlers it must be said, that while the Indians can not point to a single wrong at their hands, they have borne the wrongs and indignities heaped upon them with more than the usual ptience and forbearance of a frontier people.

Besides the facts set forth in petitions numerously signed and addressed to different authoities from whom the citizens hoped for redress, many individual cases have been brought to the knowledge of the commissioners, which leave no doubt of the increasing aggressions of the Indians upon the unresisting settlers, and that the Modocs not only prescribed the terms upon which they would permit settlements on Lost River and Rhett Lake, but in all other parts of the Modoc Basin.

To such an extent had the impudence and exactions of these usurping lords of the soil been carried, that in the fall of 1872 the settlers, dispairing of protection from the federal or state government, were banding together for self-protection; for there is every reason to believe that the first detected theft or burglary would have been followed with the summary punishment of the perpetrators, and the country involved in all the horrors of an Indian war.

The commission is aware that, in expressing an opinion of the propriety or impropriety of a military measure, it is probably extending its inquiries beyond its legitimate sphere and may seem to trench upon the prerogatives of the military, but each step, in this melancholly affair, is so intimately connected with every other that it seems the report of the commission, on this part of their inquiries, would be incomplete if this final document was omitted. Advice had been given to these Indians by white men, to evade if not resist the authority of the Indian department, and an individual (now no more) was under promise to warn them of the approach of the soldiers, should military force be resorted to. Hence, it was well known to the Indian department and colonel Green, that a military force would fail to arrest the Indians, if they were advised of the time of its coming. The unfortunate man who did not know of, but had promised to inform the Indians of the coming of the soldiers, was murdered with the rest of the unoffending settlers — another example, if more were wanting, to show that gratitude is not a prominent virtue of the savage.

FAIRCHILD'S RANCH, February 25th, 1873.

To the HON. H. R. CLUM, Acting Commissioner, etc.

The special commission to inquire into, and bring to a close the Modoc war, in reply to the second clause of its instructions, "To devise the most effective and judicious measures for preventing the continuance of these hostilities, and for the restoration of peace," have to say:

First, That in any settlement of the present hostilities with the Modocs, either to return them to the Klamath Reservation, or set apart for them a new reservation on Lost River, or in any other place in this vicinity, is now inadmissable.

Second, A peace, on the basis of general amnesty, will bring the jurisdiction of the federal and state governments in conflict, and set an example or precedent calculated to demoralize and discontent the Indians on the reservations — greatly dissatisfy the friends and neighbors of the murdered citizens, and lead speedily to Indian wars far more extensive and bloody than the one now waged with the Modocs.

Third, The commission further think that the peace most to the interest of both whites and Indians can only be secured by the removal of the Indians to some distant reservation, where the irritations growing out of the late and former conflicts between the races will not be revived by the immediate presence of the combatants, on the field of conflict.

Fourth, That the eight men indicted by the grand jury of Jackson county, Oregon, should be surrendered to the civil authorities of Oregon, *should they be demanded,* and it should be the duty of the government to assign them counsel for their defense, and see they have a fair and impartial trial, and protection from all lawless violence.

Fifth, Should the terms the commission propose to the Modocs be accepted by them, they should immediately be removed to some military post other than Fort Klamath, where they should be cared for, and kept under surveillance by the government, until their final destination shall be determined on.

The facts leading the commission to the foregoing conclusions are:

First, Before the late collision it might have been practicable to have assigned to captain Jack's band of Modocs a reservation on Lost River, and a majority of the members of the commission favored (one of them officially) such a measure, but by the annoyance and misconduct of the Indians themselves toward settlers in all parts of the Modoc Basin, as well as that part asked for by them as a reservation, had made such a concession impolitic even before the late unfortunate collision. The bitterness engendered since that time renders the naming of such a measure as one of peace, an absurdity.

To send these renegades back to the Klamath Reservation, to be kept at either Klamath or Yainax, is also out of the question. One of the excuses of captain Jack for violating his treaty stipulations is, that he could not live in peace and amity with the Klamaths, and that they used their superior strength to oppress his people. With much more justice can he now urge this objection, for, since the outbreak, not only a band of Klamath Indians from Klamath agency, but loyal Modocs from Yainax, have also acted with the troops against him. It might be a deserved punishment to send captain Jack's band to the rigorous climate of the Klamath Reservation, but it would be a deep and undeserved insult to a faithful and loyal people to make their country a kind of penal colony for thieves and brigands, with whom they are to live hereafter on terms of equality; and, in this latter objection, will be found a serious difficulty in locating the Modocs on any reservation now established. No agent, whose charge is over a peaceful and harmonious people, would care to admit them, nor will the people themselves be willing to receive such an element of vice and discord in their midst.

The reasons for the second conclusion of the commission necessarily requires a statement of the law as well as the facts of the case. The Modocs ceded their country in the most formal and absolute manner to the United States, on the 14th of October, 1864. After the ratification of the treaty by the senate, the whole Modoc tribe went and took up their abode on the reservation agreed upon in the treaty. Superintendent Meacham, *with his own hands*, distributed to them *more* than the due proportion of goods to which they were entitled by treaty. All remained and were fed at the expense of the government until the fishing season of the following spring, when captain Jack's band left the reservation without leave and has never returned to it, seeking by legal advice and every other way to evade or escape the performance of his part of the treaty, after having enjoyed its advantages. Three several times persons were sent to these people, urging them to return to their duty, and to keep their promises, ample protection from the Klamaths, and redress of their grievances being at each time promised them, but without avail. At one time the superintendent of Indian affairs for Oregon, in his earnest desire to maintain the peace, even proposed to the Indian department to set off these discontented people a reservation where they desired it, but his request was not granted. Perhaps, before the proposition was considered at Washington, these people, in disregard of their promises of good behavior, became more than ever aggressive toward the settlers, and increased their demands upon the government.

After the treaty of 1864, the government extended the public surveys over the country purchased of the Modocs. As usual, settlers followed, and even preceded the public surveys, and scattered themselves over a pastoral country too remote from each other to render mutual assistance. While the Indian department was seeking to ascertain their grievances, and seeking to redress them when found, these people were roving in bands over the country, claiming the whole of it as their own, insulting the settlers, breaking into their houses, and enforcing their demands upon them by intimidation. To put an end to this state of things, superintendent Odeneal, under an order from the department at Washington, dated July 6, 1872, to put these people back upon the reservation — "peaceably if possible, forcibly if necessary, " — repaired in person to Linkville, the nearest point to the residence of the Indians, where supplies and accommodations could be had, and invited them to meet him there and make a free and full statement of their grievances and wants, promising them ample redress. This last overture of the superintendent was not only refused, but refused with insult, even after this order was turned over to be executed by the military. The orders of colonel Green to major Jackson, in command of the force detailed to execute the order, directed him by no means to use force until more peaceful means were exhausted; and even then not to fire upon the Indians until they first fired upon him. The report of major Jackson shows that he executed his orders to the letter.

Under the auspices of superintendent Odeneal, some volunteer citizens . were raised at Linkvillee and rendezvoused at Lone Pine, about ten miles north of the Indian village, to join themselves to major Jackson's command and co-operate with it.

Major Jackson, thinking his command too small to divide, marched his whole force upon the village on the west side of Lost River, while the citizens, thirteen in number, were to be on the east side of the river simultaneously with the arrival of troops on the west. Unfortunately, this force was inadequate to the service assigned it. Had it been suffi- cient to disarm the Indians encamped on the east side and prevent others from crossing, none would have fallen on either side except those partici- pating in the struggle itself, which would have removed the most difficult complication of this unfortunate affair and made its settlement much easier.

Though the firing had commenced on the west before any hostile act was committed by either party east of the river, and the Indians were first to commence hostilities — John Thurber, a citizen, being shot and killed while in the friendly act of shaking hands — yet the Indians claim the citizens made the attack upon them because a woman and two children were killed in the melee. They plead this in justification of the murder of many citizens, neither present nor knowing of any contem- plated movement of troops likely to lead to hostilities with the Modocs. Even if all claimed by the Indians be true (and we have the assertions of several white men to the contrary), as such a plea could not be offered in extenuation of crimes so diabolical, if committed by a white man, it cannot justify Indians, to this extent quite as intelligent. But as the perpetrators were of a despised race, toward whom a deep prejudice exists in the community, the government should see that these men, against whom indictments have been found in Jackson county, if tried at all, should have able counsel and every other assistance to secure to them a fair and impartial trial — the Indians having treaty relations with the government and absent from their reservation, without leave of their agent, and committing a series of murders, robberies and burglaries on peaceful, unoffending citizens within the limits of an organized county and the jurisdiction of an independent state. The federal government can not lawfully shield these malefactors from answering for their crimes to the authorities of the state, nor should it do so. Amnesty to such offenders would be the worst possible policy, and fatal to the peace of the frontier settlements, and a serious check upon the spread of a civilized population over the yet unsubdued regions of the west.

By the whites, such conduct would be construed into a denial by the federal government of that protction to life and property to the frontier settler to which every citizens of the United States, wherever he may lawfully be, both at home and abroad, is entitled. The Indian construction would be even more erroneous and mischievous. His ruling motives spring from *interest and fear*, and he, like others, arrives at the motives of others by comparing them with his own. The magnanimity of the government is by him mistaken for fear. So long as a perverted sympathy and mawkish sentimentality elevates an Indian murderer into a hero, great according to the greatness and atrocity of his crimes, and the representatives of the government bestow more attention and respect upon its enemies than its friends, and the shortest road to its notice and favor is by shedding innocent blood, we will not soon see an end of Indian atrocities, nor the government, without frequent opportunity to exercise a mischievous lenity calculated to encourage crime at the expense of innocence.

The remaining conclusions, of the commission, being sequents of those already explained, need no extended explanation. Should the state of Oregon demand for trial those accused of the murder of its citizens, as wards of the government, the government is, in duty bounnd, to see that their trial shall be fair and impartial, and according to law.

The details necessary to carry into effect the foregoing conclusions, and to provide for the future of these Indians, the commission consider beyond the scope of their duties to recommend.